Good Morning Loon

It's Early Morning–What's Happening on the Lake?

By Elizabeth S. Varnai

Illustrated by Kate Hartley

Vista Court Books
New Hope, Pennsylvania

It's early morning ...

Text © 2014 by Elizabeth S. Varnai
Illustrations © 2014 by Kate Hartley
Book design by Sheri Amsel

Library of Congress Control Number: 2013930875
ISBN 978-0-9628422-3-8

Publisher's Cataloging-in-Publication Data:
Varnai, Elizabeth S.
  Good morning loon : it's early morning : what's happening on the lake? / by Elizabeth S. Varnai ; illustrated by Kate Hartley.
    pages cm
    Includes bibliographical references. Fuller descriptions of wildlife follow text.
  SUMMARY: On a summer morning, a boy and his mother set out to canoe a northern lake. What is splashing in the marsh grasses? Swimming toward them? Flying above? Will they see a loon? Discoveries and surprises await.
    Audience: Ages 4-8.
    LCCN 2013930875
    ISBN 978-0-9628422-3-8 (hardback)
1. Animals--Juvenile fiction. 2. Loons--Juvenile fiction. 3. Nature stories--Juvenile fiction. 4. Mothers and sons--Juvenile fiction. 5. Canoes and canoeing--Juvenile fiction. 6. Adirondack Mountains (N.Y.)--Juvenile fiction. [1. Animals--Fiction. 2. Loons--Fiction. 3. Nature stories--Fiction. 4. Mothers and sons--Fiction. 5. Canoes and canoeing--Fiction. 6. Adirondack Mountains (N.Y.)--Fiction.]   I. Hartley, Kate (Katherine M.), illustrator. II. Title.
  PZ7.V4432Goo 2014

Printed by Versa Press, East Peoria, IL U.S.A
Printed in May 2014

10 9 8 7 6 5 4

Vista Court Books
P.O. Box 277
New Hope, PA 18938-0227
www.vistacourtbooks.com

I open my eyes.
Good morning, sun!
It's time to get up—
we're going canoeing
this morning!

Mom is waiting for me, smiling.

"Are you ready?" she asks.

"Yes! I'm ready!"

We start down the path
to the lake.

We hear rustling and chattering—

CH-CH-CH-CH-CH! What is it?

A red squirrel scurrying away.

A little farther Mom stops. "We almost missed it."

"Look closely," she says. "Do you see the wood frog?"

We reach the lake while the morning mist is still rising.

Good morning, canoe!

We put on our life jackets and set out
along the shore.

"Will we see a loon?" I ask.
"If we are very, very lucky," Mom
replies.

In the grasses, we hear splish-splashing.

Mom whispers: "A family of mergansers!"

We paddle on. The water ripples. A brown head appears.

A beaver!

CHURR ... CHURR ... CHURR!

Good morning, beaver!

Mom says, "Maybe it's telling us, DON'T GET TOO CLOSE!"

"Maybe we did get too close," says Mom. "We'd better move away."

KNOCK—KNOCK—KNOCK ...

KNOCK—KNOCK

Who's there?

"Wow, it's big! What kind of woodpecker is that?"

"A pileated woodpecker," Mom tells me.

"See the big hole it's chipping? It's looking for ants to eat."

Ahead lies an island. "What's on top of the tree?"

"An osprey's nest," Mom replies.
"But it looks empty. Where is the osprey?"

THERE – bringing home a fish!
The osprey's chicks reach up,
eager for their breakfast.

The nest isn't empty after all.

We paddle toward a big rock.

What will we see on the other side?

A great blue heron!

Good morning! What are you doing?

"He's hunting for breakfast," Mom explains.

"When he spots a fish or a frog, he'll grab it!"

We paddle away from shore.

So far, no loon.

We meet another canoe.

"Good morning, fisherman," I say.

"Did you catch anything?"

"Not yet," he replies.

"Have you seen a loon?"

"Not yet," he says again, "but I heard one."

A visitor lands on our canoe.

Good morning, dragonfly!

"This dragonfly is called a twelve-spotted skimmer," Mom tells me.

"Can you count the spots on its wings?"

SPLASH!

"A trout!" Mom says.

"Be careful, trout," I say, "there's a fisherman nearby!"

AhOOO ... AhOOO ... AhOOO

A loon!

Where is it?

"There!"

Mom points to a black shape far away.

The loon dives underwater.

It must be hungry! Somewhere below, it's chasing a fish.

We wait.

When will it come up? And where?

It's HERE!

GOOD MORNING, LOON, GOOD MORNING!

The sun is higher now. The mist has lifted.

I'm getting hungry, too.

"Let's paddle back," Mom says.

"It's time for OUR breakfast."

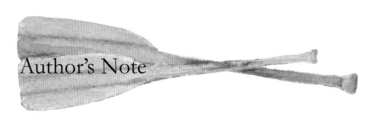

Author's Note

This story is based on experiences I've enjoyed while paddling on lakes in the Adirondack Mountains in northern New York State. Similar lakes can be found in other northern regions, for example, in New England, the Upper Midwest, and Canada.

While paddling on such northern lakes, you might encounter some of the creatures shown in this book. Or, you might see other wildlife. Wood ducks may be gliding along in a marsh. A mink may scurry along a shore. Deer may come to the water's edge for a drink.

You never know what you will see. Sometimes, the creatures are hiding and all seems quiet. Other times, you can be surprised by a creature you haven't seen before.

Always, you can enjoy watching for what may appear on the shore, on or in the water, and what flies above.

Thank you to …

• Interpretive Naturalist Kendra Ormerod and her colleagues at The Wild Center (Natural History Museum of the Adirondacks) in Tupper Lake, New York. Their reviews of the manuscript for accuracy and their advice on which creatures are likely to be seen, or not, at certain times of the year were invaluable.

• Zoologist Erin White for her special expertise in dragonflies, developed through her work with the New York Natural Heritage Program, a partnership between the New York State Department of Environmental Conservation and the State University of New York College of Environmental Science and Forestry.

• To Eva, Heidi, Lesl, Anika, and Krista, who advised on the manuscript from their child's point of view; and to Clayton for posing.

To all who generously share their love and knowledge of the natural world.

Tell me more ...

Red squirrel. Larger than a chipmunk but smaller than a gray squirrel, the red squirrel lives in forests of pine, fir, and spruce trees. It eats the trees' seeds and cones, as well as insects, fruits, and mushrooms it finds in the forest. If you walk through an evergreen forest, you may hear one chattering and screeching, or see one scurrying up a tree trunk, or scampering from branch or branch. On the ground, you may see one hurrying from bush to bush looking for cover against predators like foxes or like owls that might swoop down from above.

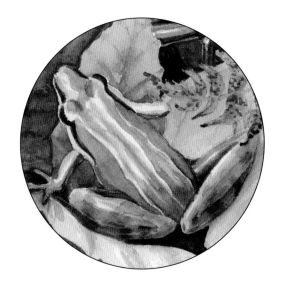

Wood frog. You might not notice a wood frog until it hops, because its coloring blends with the forest floor. This helps it hide from predators. Wood frogs are active in warm weather, when they look for insects, worms, and slugs to eat. When cold weather comes, they settle under rocks or dig into decaying leaves. They don't have to dig deep, though. Even if they freeze like an ice cube, they can thaw out.

Common merganser. The merganser is a large duck that swims on clear lakes and rivers with wooded shores. It has a long, narrow, red bill with serrated edges to help it catch and hold fish. Female mergansers have a reddish-brown tufted head and a grayish body. Males look very different, with a greenish-black head and black and white body. In northern areas, female mergansers lay their eggs in May and June and incubate their eggs for about five weeks.

After hatching, baby mergansers can leave the nest within one or two days, ready to swim and find their own food, such as water insects, tadpoles, and small fish. Mergansers like to travel in groups. They may swim with not only their own family, but with others as well. You might see many mergansers swimming in a line, some dipping underwater with little splashes to snatch a fish.

Beaver. If you see a mound of branches along a shore, you are probably seeing the top of a beaver's home or "lodge." Beavers enter their lodge underwater, then climb up inside to a dry space. For food, beavers gnaw at trees until they fall, then strip off their bark and small branches to eat. Beavers use leftover sticks and branches to build their lodges and dams. When dams or lodges are built along a stream, they often change its course or create wetlands. The beaver's body is well suited for life on both land and water. Its webbed feet help it swim. Its broad, flat tail helps it balance when it is sitting or standing, and also helps it steer while swimming. When a beaver senses danger, it slams the water hard with its tail as a warning, making a loud slapping sound and big splash.

Pileated woodpecker. These large woodpeckers, which grow up to 19 inches long, live in older forests where there are many dead standing trees and fallen logs. They use their powerful beaks to chip out large rectangular holes in search of ants, their favorite food. If you see a large rectangular hole, you know a pileated woodpecker has been there.

Osprey. Ospreys eat only fish, so they live near lakes and saltwater bays, building nests on top of dead trees or poles. If you see an osprey flying high above a lake or bay, it is probably looking for fish with its keen eyes. When it spots one, it dives feet first, even going underwater to catch the fish with its talons. A pair of adult ospreys may have one to three chicks in a season, but often not all survive. While the chicks are very young, it is the male osprey that hunts and brings fish to the nest. After about six weeks, the chicks learn to fly and begin to hunt on their own. Then, the female begins hunting, too. She hunts for herself and for her chicks until the young can hunt well enough to completely feed themselves.

Great blue heron. You might see this tall long-legged, long-necked bird stepping slowly through shallow water or perched on a branch near the water. It can also stand as still as a statue, waiting for prey like small fish and frogs to swim by, then striking lightning-fast. You can find great blue herons along the shores of ponds, lakes, on riverbanks, and in fresh or saltwater marshes.

Trout. This is a brook trout, a native to cold, clear streams and lakes in the eastern half of North America. You can identify a brook trout by the wavy lines on its body and the large yellow spots and smaller red spots in a blue halo along its sides. Similar to other trout, it eats small fish, insects and almost anything else in or on the water that fits into its mouth. It can also leap into the air to catch an insect flying above the water.

Dragonfly. This dragonfly is called a twelve-spotted skimmer because of the number of brown spots on its wings. Other dragonflies are larger, or smaller, or have jewel-colored bodies and different patterns on their wings. But all have large eyes and two pairs of wings held outstretched from their long body. Dragonflies spend most of their lives underwater as nymphs. While there, they eat insect eggs, tadpoles, and aquatic invertebrates. These are creatures with no backbones that live underwater (like aquatic worms and the larvae of flies) or on top of the water (like beetles and water striders).

Once dragonflies' wings are almost fully formed, they crawl out of the water, shed their skin, wait for their soft wings to harden, and take flight. From then on, dragonflies become fast, agile predators of flying insects like mosquitoes and flies. They can zoom backwards, forwards, hover, and make quick turns.

Dragonflies' bodies must be warm before they can fly. Some need the warmth of the sun to fly and be active. If you see a dragonfly perched on a branch, a log, or even the bow of a canoe, it may be pausing to absorb the sun's heat. Other dragonflies, like darners, can warm themselves up by making their flight muscles shiver and by vibrating their wings as they perch. These rapid motions create heat that spreads through the dragonfly's body, allowing it to be active in cooler temperatures or cooler months.

Common loon. If you go canoeing on a clear northern lake, an "ahOOO" call may be the first sign that a loon is near. Adult loons eat only fish, diving and swimming underwater to catch them. With their powerful webbed feet, they can swim long distances, holding their breath for up to 60 seconds or more. In the late fall, when ice begins to form, loons fly south to seacoasts or large lakes that don't freeze over.

You can listen to the different calls of a loon at **loon.org**.

Tell me EVEN more …
Here are some of the many resources available to learn more:

Books
Fiona A. Reid, Peterson Field Guide Staff, *Mammals of North America: Field Guide*, Houghton Mifflin Harcourt, 2006.

David Allen Sibley, *The Sibley Field Guide to Birds of Eastern North America*, Alfred A. Knopf, Inc., 2003.

James P. Gibbs, Alvin R. Breisch et al, *The Amphibians and Reptiles of New York State: Identification, Natural History, and Conservation*, Oxford University Press, 2007.

Websites
DEC.ny.gov

Dnr.state.mn.us

Animaldiversity.ummz.umich.edu

Biokids.umich.edu

Allaboutbirds.org

Exploringnature.org